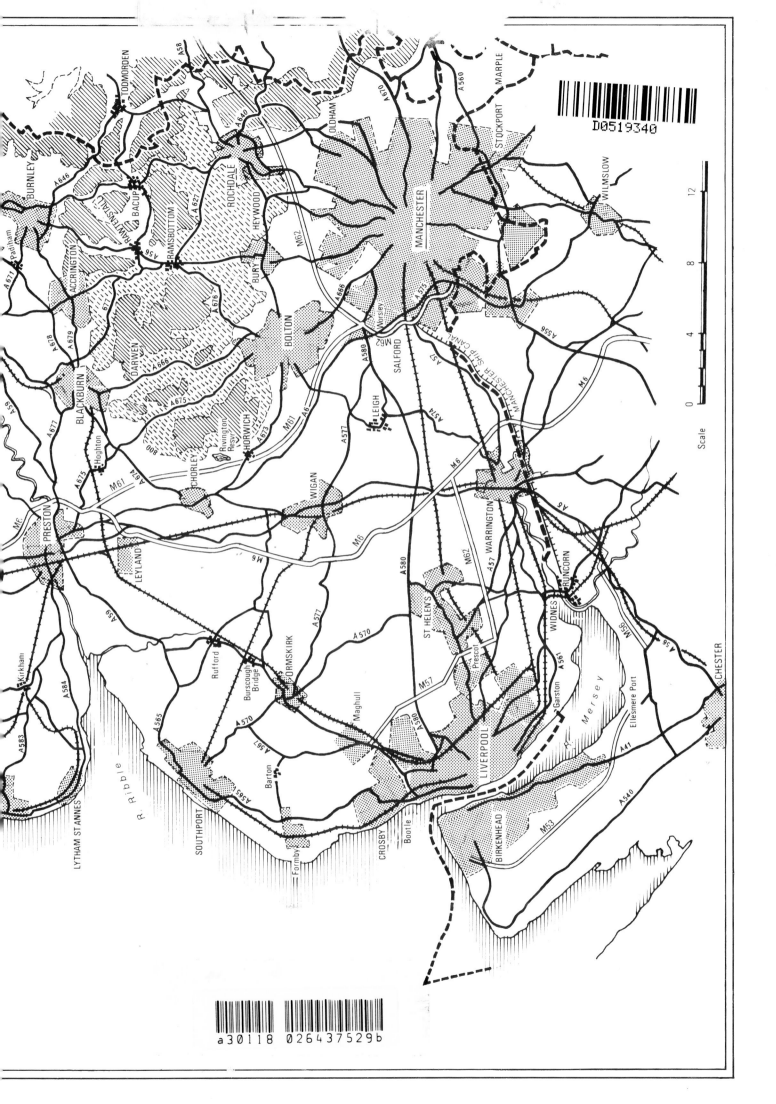

D0519340

a30118 026437529b

# England in cameracolour
# Lancashire

# England in cameracolour
# Lancashire

Photographs by F. A. H. BLOEMENDAL
Text by NESTA ROBERTS

Town & County BOOKS

483125898

L000264903
02643752

## Bibliography

*The Buildings of England: South Lancashire* and *North Lancashire*, edited Nikolaus Pevsner; Penguin Books

*Lancashire*, J. J. Bagley; Batsford

*The King's England: Lancashire*, Arthur Mee; Hodder & Stoughton

*Red Guide: The Lake District*; Ward Lock & Co Ltd

*Walking in the Lake District*, H. H. Symonds; W. & R. Chambers Ltd

*Around Morecambe Bay*, W. R. Mitchell; The Dalesman

*Explore Lancashire by Car*, Jane Sterling; The Dalesman

*Lancaster*, Derek James; The Dalesman

First published 1983

ISBN 0 86364 010 9

All rights reserved. No part of this book may be
reproduced or transmitted in any form or by any
means, electronic or mechanical, including photo-
copying, recording or by any information storage
and retrieval system, without permission from the
Publisher in writing.

Photographs © F. A. H. Bloemendal 1983

© Town & County Books Ltd 1983

Published by Town & County Books Ltd, Shepperton, Surrey;
and printed in Italy by Athesia Druck Gmbh, Bozen

# Introduction

'The Queen — the Duke of Lancaster', they say when they raise their glasses for the loyal toast in Lancashire, and newcomers who query what they take to be a local eccentricity are sent back to their history books. The Queen, which is to say the reigning monarch, *is* the Duke of Lancaster, and has been since 1399, when Henry of Hereford, son of John of Gaunt, who had inherited the title from his father, came to the throne as Henry IV. Instead of absorbing his dukedom into his kingdom the new monarch enlarged its territory and maintained its palatinate powers. To this day Lancashire retains a few survivals of its old administrative autonomy: the Chancellor of the Duchy of Lancaster does not hold a purely ornamental office.

A proud county, then, and an independent one, but perhaps more often and more thoroughly traduced than any other in Britain. Most places suffer from misconceptions ('It always rains in the Highlands', 'All Lincolnshire is as flat as the back of your hand', 'These days Essex is just London overspill') but for few are they as wholesale as for Lancashire. The entire Palatinate is envisaged as a gigantic Lowry landscape dominated by dark satanic mills.

The truth is that, since the Industrial Revolution, there have been two Lancashires, one urban, one rural, in parts even wild. In size the county ranks seventh in the country; in population it is first except for London, and two-thirds of that population is crowded into one quarter of the area. South Lancashire is as intensively industrialised as the Ruhr; in the north there are places where one can be a mainland Crusoe. The eastern moors border on the wild Brontë country; on the west coast the Irish Sea creeps in over the deserted flats of Morecambe Bay.

Three hundred years ago the only contrasts were geographical, those between the coastal plain — there is no drama in the Lancashire coastline, though there is ample interest — and the Pennines and their outliers that form the border with Yorkshire, between the valley farmland and the upland sheep runs. The county's remoteness meant that a good deal of history passed it by, or passed over it lightly. From pre-history we have, most notably, the decorated Calderstones, now in Liverpool Museum, which were found in a passage grave, and a funerary monument at Bleasdale, where the site of the original timber posts which surrounded a barrow are now marked by concrete pillars. The Romans came to control but not to settle on the scale that they did in the south; there were forts in Lancashire but few if any villas. The native Celts, the Brigantes, watched Agricola's legions on the march from Manchester or Chester up to Hadrian's Wall, but seem to have been little disturbed in their own way of life. Later, as place names tell us, the Norsemen, using Ireland as a jumping-off place, penetrated from the west and the Saxons from the east. Christianity came early, probably also from Ireland, and survived. The Normans were brutal in their suppression of the northerners who rebelled against the Conquest, though they later made some amends by founding religious houses at Lancaster and Furness. Cartmel (Plate 44) came later, under the Plantagenets, and it was they, too, who granted many of the charters which witness to the ancient past of industrial towns. The distance of this north-western region from the centre of government helped to ensure that 'the old religion' was not extinguished by the Reformation. If the Roman Church is strong in Lancashire today it is only partly due to Irish immigration. The other element is the faithfulness of the many local great families and their dependents, who maintained a passive, and sometimes active resistance to Anglicanism. Those pockets of Romanism tended to be Royalist during the Civil War and Jacobite during the later bids for the throne of the Old and Young Pretender.

At the time of the rebellion of 1745 Lancashire was still sparsely populated. Then, as now, Manchester was the largest town, but its population was only 5,000. Most people still earned their living from the land, by farming or stock-breeding, though, since the 15th century, there had been some growth of small industries, metal work, spinning and weaving, open cast coal mining, often carried on as a secondary occupation.

The transformation — it is tempting to call it an explosion, in the word's proper sense of a sudden release of energy — began in the 18th century and continued through the 19th. Power-driven machinery increased the scale of production astronomically, turned the cottage craftsmen into factory hands and brought the agricultural workers into the towns. The kind of internal migration that Spain, Italy and even France have experienced in our own day began in Lancashire around the turn of the 18th and 19th centuries. A network of canals which 5 produced staggering feats of engineering gave the county a transport system that was almost as important a factor in its prosperity as steam power, and, as early as the end of the 17th century, the building of a number of locks in the Mersey below Warrington foreshadowed the Ship Canal which, almost exactly 200 years later, was to make Manchester a major port. The first public passenger railway in the world was that from Liverpool to Manchester, opened in 1830.

The result of this seemingly uncontrollable industrial growth was a ravaged landscape, dreadful housing and sanitation that was absent rather than poor. In the early part of the 19th century Manchester and Liverpool knew the kind of epidemics of cholera, typhoid and typhus which, today, we associate with Calcutta. At least the county was energetic in combating those ills. Lancashire's long list of 'firsts', Free Trade and free libraries and the first wet dock, as well as canals and railways, can claim also the first medical officer of health (MOH) in Britain and the first district nursing service, both in Liverpool.

It is natural that holidaymakers today should turn towards the north of the county, but if they do not spare two or three days for the south they will miss a rare experience. Two hundred years of our history, an epoch that had an almost Elizabethan energy and confidence, is written in these mill chimneys, no longer plumed with smoke, these docks, some of which are officially or virtually maritime museums, in stretches of canal whose surface is disturbed only by anglers. To walk the streets of Manchester and Liverpool with a copy of Mrs Gaskell's *North and South* in one's pocket is to learn more of our fairly recent past than is likely to be absorbed in quite a number of lessons in economics and social history.

Between them, the two cities illustrate when the money came into the area and how nobly much of it was spent. One does not go to either to see ancient buildings; indeed Lancashire as whole is not rich in medieval magnificence. There are exceptions of course, the black and white Speke Hall a reminder on the industrial edge of Liverpool that once the county was well-wooded and timber houses were the norm, Manchester Cathedral (Plate 106), with its neighbour, the 15th century buildings of Chetham's Hospital, great houses like Stonyhurst, or Rufford Old Hall. There are others, but mostly the fine buildings, like the money, date from the 18th and 19th centuries, and sometimes, as happened in Liverpool, the improvements that came with prosperity destroyed some of the evidence of the past. War damage accounted for some more.

Manchester made the goods in which Liverpool traded, and her manufacturers built warehouses like Italian palazzi and went on to build libraries and museums and art galleries like, or approximately like Greek temples. In the mid-19th century they built the Free Trade Hall — it had had two predecessors, one temporary, one brick and scarcely worthy, to commemorate the success of the Anti-Corn Law League, and, in the mid-20th they rebuilt it after bomb damage to be a permanent home of the glorious Hallé Orchestra. Above all, they built a Town Hall which, in its ornateness and the mastery of its craftsmanship, is the very epitome of Victorian architecture. It is hard to raise even two cheers for some of the sad curtain walling which has recently gone up in the centre of Manchester, which accords neither with the massive grey stone blocks of Mosley Street and Portland Street nor with the extravaganza in Albert Square.

Liverpool, only 35 miles distant, is radically different. From the first the port, tiny as it was in the 13th century when the city received its first charter, has been its *raison d'être*, and to this day the Mersey estuary, coming down broad and brimming into the Irish Sea, gives the city an air of exhilaration. A young woman who stayed at Blackpool in 1788, when it was a secluded bathing resort, spoke of meeting 'Manchesterians reserved and purse-proud' and 'Liverpoolians free and open as the sea on which they get their riches'. That may be hard on Manchester, a notably warm-hearted city, but it does express the lavish generosity which was typical of Liverpool. The city raised enough money by public subscription to put up, in St George's Hall (Plate 18), one of the finest public buildings in Europe, the splendid museum, library and art gallery in William Brown Street are a memorial to private benefactions; a merchant saw no contradiction between earning money in the slave trade and spending it on endowing a school for poor boys. The banks and insurance offices and the headquarters of the great shipping companies are sumptuous, even the interiors of the pubs recall a luxury liner. And now Liverpool has built itself not one, but two cathedrals.

Inland, scattered to the north and north-west of Manchester, there is a group of textile towns, Bolton, Rochdale, Bury, Burnley, Blackburn, Preston, which are as expressive of a merchant, as distinct from an aristocratic culture as is, say, Amsterdam. Rochdale and Bolton have town halls of a grandeur that compares with those of Flemish cities, all spent generously on museums and art galleries, and, like Manchester and Liverpool, all laid out parks. In passing, it is worth noting that even the least attractive of the industrial towns of south Lancashire has more and shorter escape routes to the open country than most comparable areas in London and the Midlands.

Finally, to understand industrial Lancashire, one must go to the seaside, or rather, to two seasides, for a greater gulf than the Ribble estuary divides Southport from Blackpool. Both grew with the cotton boom and the craze for sea-bathing, but they grew in different directions, Southport into leisured gentility, with boulevards and lawns and gardens, with a splendid golf course at Birkdale as a bonus, Blackpool (Plate 28) into the most vital and ebullient seaside resort in the country. A hundred years ago the *Morning Post* told its readers that Blackpool offered 'more fun for less money than anywhere else'. It is fun of the hearty kind, and even the air conspires to invigorate visitors.

Rural Lancashire begins almost immediately north of the cotton towns, for it is a short enough step from Blackburn, or Burnley or Nelson to the moors, the good farmland around Pendle, the smiling upper valley of the Ribble and even the wild country of the Trough of Bowland (Plate 72). But in spirit one enters it further north-west, at Lancaster (Plate 36), the county town, where the castle that the Normans built on the height above the river still dominates the town and the church beside it had its beginnings as that of an 11th century Benedictine priory. The domestic architecture is largely Georgian, and of good grey stone. A few miles outside the town one can see the face of the future in the buildings of the post-war university, which were designed in the 1960s.

Arcadia lies north of Lancaster. Once Morecambe, which, as seaside towns go, may be described as 'Blackpool type', has been left behind, and one has shut one's eyes to Carnforth, a railway town which is even less interesting than the average railway town, one can choose between small, peaceful resorts like Silverdale (Plate 40) and the Yealands, Arnside and Grange-over-Sands, some no more than villages, all individually interesting, and the solitary stretches on the shores of Morecambe Bay. This is a unique and entrancing marine landscape, with its endless miles of green and glitter, where sand and shallows and salt marsh alternate and intermingle. Companies of seabirds patrol it, and, northward, the ramparts of the Lakeland mountains block the horizon.

The Furness Peninsula on the far side of the bay is another country where, in a small compass, one can move from the ship-building town of Barrow (Plate 62), one of the very few, if not the only town born of the Industrial Revolution which was deliberately planned, to the impressive ruins of the once great abbey of Furness. Off the tip of the peninsula there is a scatter of islands of which one, Piel, in fact the only true island, as the rest are linked with the mainland by bridges or causeways, has the remains of an early 14th century castle which the monks of Furness built to guard the coast against Scottish invaders.

Wordsworth's Lake District is scarcely 15 miles north of Piel Island, and not Wordsworth's alone, though his is the abiding presence. Poets and prosewriters congregated among these hills, Southey and Coleridge and de Quincey, Ruskin and Harriet Martineau, not to mention Mrs Hemans, who wrote *The boy stood on the burning deck*. The road skirts Coniston Water, with the Old Man, the highest point in Lancashire, rising on the left. Windermere (Plate 48) is over the fells to the right; ahead the view is lordly, with the piled up ranges of the Langdale Pikes and Helvellyn in the distance. Let us stop at Hawkshead, which is near enough to the county boundary to be taken as a frontier post. The church on the hill looks down on the roofs of the village, whose white houses and many friendly pubs, threaded by a maze of lanes and tunnels, face inwards, not in exclusiveness but in deserved self-content. Over the porch of the Grammar School (Plate 52) the dial that Wordsworth knew still marks only the sunny hours. Wigan and Widnes, Manchester and Bolton and even Morecambe are a thousand miles away, but here, too, they raise their glasses to 'The Queen, the Duke of Lancaster'.

*Nesta Roberts,*
*1983*   7

*Runcorn Bridge, Widnes* What drama! What elegance! Few entries into a county offer such stark contrasts as the Runcorn bridges, road and rail, over the Mersey, by which travellers are whisked into the heart of industrial Lancashire while the buttercup meadows of Cheshire are fresh in their minds. The iron railway bridge, its great stone pylons built as massive as a Border fortress, has been there for more than a hundred years. The lovely arc of the road bridge beside it, with the carriageway suspended from its single span, was built in 1956-61 to replace a transporter bridge which had served travellers since 1905. In its day it was a popular tourist sight. The new bridge, when it was built, was the largest steel arch in Europe and the third largest in the world. The records are lost: the beauty remains.

*Liverpool - from Birkenhead Docks* The first and last of England for unnumbered Atlantic voyagers during the first half of the present century, Liverpool's waterfront remains a monument to Edwardian confidence and prosperity. If, for some contemporary critics, the architecture is slightly hammy, even they usually agree that it is extremely good ham. On the left the Liver building is claimed to be the first on its scale in the world to be constructed of reinforced concrete, here faced with granite. The Liver birds on top are no mythical monsters but authentic cormorants. Next to it the Cunard Line modelled its head office on the Farnese Palace in Rome. The green-domed Port of Liverpool building further to the right is equally a palace. Contemporary Liverpool appears on the further skyline, with, dead centre, the 450ft beacon of the Tower Restaurant and, further left, the slender diadem of the Roman Catholic cathedral.

*Liverpool Cathedral* Only Durham has a site to compare with that of Liverpool's Anglican cathedral whose ruddy sandstone mass, set on the rock of St James's Mount, dominates the city and the estuary. It is the largest Anglican church in the world and certainly the last that will be built in this country by traditional methods. Gilbert Scott was only 22 years old when his drawings were chosen from those submitted by 103 architects. Building began in 1904 and continued over 74 years, slowed but never stopped by two world wars. During the 59 years for which Scott supervised the work he revised his original plans, but the finished building remains a monument of 19th-20th century Gothic. When the Queen attended the service of dedication in 1978 the future had already arrived in the shape of its friendly neighbour at the other end of Hope Street, the audacious and exhilarating RC cathedral.

12

*Rodney Street, Liverpool* Liverpool's first
Charter came in 1207 from King John, who
thought the muddy pool with a tiny fishing
village beside it would make a base from
which he could send troops to Ireland, but it
was slow to grow. Prosperity came with the
development of the West Indian and
Virginian trade from the 17th century, first
sugar, tobacco and cotton, later slaves. The
town's handsome Georgian terraces date
mostly from the latter part of the 18th
century. Rodney Street, Liverpool's Harley
Street, which was built in brick while later
streets were of ashlar, was the first as well
as one of the best of them, with fine
doorways and pretty balconies on the first
floor. Mr Gladstone was born at No 62 and
Arthur Hugh Clough at No 9.

*Picton Library and Walker Art Gallery, Liverpool* Nineteenth century civic pride and civic prosperity produced nothing finer than the grand sweep of Liverpool's William Brown Street, whose classical buildings were conceived to accord with the masterpiece of St George's Hall, opposite, and do not shame it. The Picton Library, with a circular colonnade said to have been modelled on the Roman Pantheon, was designed by a local architect, Cornelius Sherlock. With the Hornby Library behind, and the adjoining Brown Library, it claims to have more books on open access than any other library in the country. The Walker Art Gallery next to it, the gift to his city of a former Mayor of Liverpool, Sir Andrew Barclay Walker, houses a representative collection, with a strong line in what may be called 'calendar pictures' which almost rank as folk art. They include: *When did you last see your father?*

16

*Stable Fountain and St George's Hall, Liverpool* In 1836 Liverpool, growing rapidly in size and importance, decided that it needed a worthy concert hall and, after raising £23,350 by means of a subscription fund, announced an open competition for plans for a hall which would cost £30,000. A year later it was made an assize town and another competition was organised for a court to be built on an adjoining site. Harry Lonsdale Elmes, who won both competitions, was 24 years old. He was commissioned to combine his schemes in a building that would accommodate court and concert hall. He gave the city the finest neo-classical building in Europe, whose interior is as distinguished as the noble exterior. Its young architect never saw it completed. When it was opened in 1854 Elmes had been dead for nine years.

*Leeds & Liverpool Canal, Burscough Bridge*
'The future progress of the county is beyond the reach of calculation' wrote a late 18th century topographer when he surveyed the network of canals which had given Lancashire what was considered to be a perfect transport system. It was one of the most important factors in the rapid development of South Lancashire from a rural area with a scattered population to one which was densely industrialised. Before the coming of the railways the canal boats carried passengers as well as goods. Burscough was one of the stages on the voyage of the Wigan Packet, which left Liverpool every morning at 8am, Mondays excepted. At a maximum speed of four mph, the journey to Wigan took eight hours. There was a cook on board to sustain the passengers with roasts, chops and steaks, meat pies, bacon and eggs and the like.

20

*River Yarrow, Croston* Industrial Lancashire seems distant indeed from Croston, where the single arch of a bridge spans the Yarrow and a 15th century church stands beside it. The village is at the centre of a green and tranquil area, rich in historic houses. Bretherton, a couple of miles north-west, has the early 17th century Carr House, where, in 1639, the young astronomer, Joseph Horrocks, observed the transit of Venus. Mawdesley Hall, due south of Croston, of about the same period, has a chapel in the loft — the Reformation was late in reaching remote Lancashire, which remained faithful to the Roman Church in face of Tudor and Stuart persecution. The jewel of them all is Rufford Old Hall, the home of the Heskeths, a magnificent 15th century timbered house, now owned by the National Trust.

*Harris Museum and Art Galley, Preston*
Lancashire's oldest borough, 'proud Preston' has much to be proud about in addition to its handsome museum and art gallery built in the 1880s. Foremost is the merchant guild established by the Charter of 1175, whose members enjoyed the rights of free trade. Every 20 years the borough celebrates it with a week of ceremony and festivity. During the 18th and early 19th centuries, Preston was something of a provincial capital where the country gentry had their town houses. The cotton industry blossomed after Richard Arkwright set up his spinning machine; in the present century Preston's port on the Ribble has grown in importance. The poet Francis Thompson was born here in 1859 and the temperance movement in 1830. And every Easter Monday thousands of Preston children go 'pace egging', rolling painted eggs down a slope in Avenham Park.

*Windmill on Lytham Green, Lytham St Anne's* 'One circumstance must above all others render Lytham dear to those who have a strict regard to morality — vice has not yet erected her standard here', wrote an 18th century visitor, and, even today, there is a culture shock involved in the short journey from the robust gaieties of Blackpool to the staider pleasures of Lytham St Anne's. The municipal borough falls into two parts. St Anne's is a typical late Victorian-Edwardian resort, with fine shopping streets. Lytham is mentioned in the Domesday Book, but the present town began its development at the end of the 18th century and has retained some Regency houses. The windmill on the wide green looking over the Ribble Estuary was built in 1805 by Richard Cookson, who used parts taken from disused local mills. Its sails have not turned since 1918, when the machinery was damaged in a fire.

*Blackpool Illuminations* Between seven and eight million holidaymakers visit Blackpool every year, and a sizeable number of them come in the autumn, when other resorts have battened down until the spring. They are attracted by the famous illuminations, which were devised in the hope of extending the season, and have succeeded so amply in doing so that Blackpool is in business from Easter to the end of October. Every year new features are introduced into the glitter-show which turns the sea front into a seven-mile psychedelic experience, and evening trips bring visitors from many parts of the North to 'walk the lights'.

*Tower and Central Pier, Blackpool* Blackpool's tower was opened in 1894, five years after the Eiffel Tower, on which it was avowedly modelled, though it is not much more than half the height, 518ft 9in to the flagstaff. The lifts average 50,000 trips a year, and it is well worth taking one of them to enjoy a panorama of the resort which represents the other half of the Industrial Revolution. 'Workers' Playtime' was a phrase which had not come into the language when Blackpool set out to give the many all they could wish for during their brief annual holiday. From 500ft up one has it all at one's feet, the biggest ballroom and the most hectic amusement park, the piers and gardens and promenades and swimming pools and golf courses, and, beyond, the miles of sands and the sea that the winds of winter bring crashing over the promenade.

*Fleetwood* A 19th century new town, Fleetwood was envisaged by its begetter, Sir Peter Kesketh Fleetwood, in 1837, as 'a resort in the style of Brighton or St Leonard's, which would combine the advantages of a Commercial Port with those of a Watering Place'. He engaged Decimus Burton, the disciple of John Nash, to lay it out among the dunes at the tip of the Wyre peninsula. Barton's concept is preserved in the broad streets radiating from the focal point of The Mount, the gracious houses of Queen's Terrace and the curving façade of the North Euston Hotel, where railway travellers spent the night after the first stage of their journey from London to Scotland. But the new railway over Shap made the staging post unnecessary. Blackpool attracted more holidaymakers and Sir Peter lost his all, or virtually so. Today Fleetwood, if not a northern Brighton, is a quieter alternative to Blackpool, with the added interest of being a fishing port.

32

*Canal Locks near Thurnham* There is a little Holland in the area around Thurnham, particularly to the south. The level, fertile fields were reclaimed from the peat mosses; drainage ditches quarter them and the roads run on embankments above. The locks pictured are on the extension of the Lancaster Canal to Glasson Dock. It was not completed until 1826, too late to reverse the decline in Lancaster's trade, as had been hoped. By then Glasson Dock, built with the same object, had been operational for more than 30 years. It was projected as a major port and was equipped with a wet dock for 25 merchant ships, one of the earliest in the country, but it, too, declined with Lancashire. Today only pleasure sailing craft, with the occasional coaster, put in at Glasson.

*Lancaster* Lancaster has been described as an 18th century town with a medieval street plan. It was mentioned in Domesday, and, long before that, was a Roman fort. Its first charter was granted by King John, and Roger de Pôitou, who built its castle around 1100, also gave it a Benedictine house which was the earliest monastery in Lancashire. The picture shows one of the dignified grey streets in the foreground and, in the distance, a later addition to the townscape. The domed building on the skyline is the Ashton Memorial, known locally as 'the structure', which is possibly Britain's nearest approach to the Taj Mahal — in intention if not in architecture. It was built by James, later Lord Ashton, of the family who established the linoleum trade in Lancaster, in memory of his first wife. The view from its 150ft dome is even more impressive than that from the castle.

*Old Custom House, Lancaster*  The Old Custom House, whose Palladian portico adorns St George's quay, is a reminder of Lancaster's brief 'Golden Age', which gave the town its many good Georgian buildings. From about 1740 to 1800 its port had a share in the West Indies trade, slavery included, which, small though it was compared with that of London, Liverpool and Bristol, brought prosperity to the local merchants. Many of them imported mahogany with which the town's cabinetmakers produced fine furniture, some for the great houses of England, some for re-export to the planters of the islands. One of the founders of that industry, Robert Gillow, started out as a maker of pig troughs, mangles and coffins. It was his son, Richard, trained as an architect, who designed and built the Custom House.

*Silverdale* Silverdale, like its neighbour, Arnside, is almost a specific antidote for Morecambe and Blackpool — a peaceful, scattered village which has attracted many writers. Mrs Gaskell did much of her best work here, and, in her leisure hours, loved to watch the great sunsets over Morecambe Bay from the summit of the tower built in the early 19th century by a banker named Fleetwood. These days Silverdale can scarcely claim to be a seaside resort since the wandering channel of the River Kent is having one of its periods of moving further from the shore, so that only the highest tides cover the grass flats. In summer there are acres of sea thrift in bloom between Silverdale and Arnside and the whole area is rich in the wild flowers of limestone country.

40

*Market Cross and Priory Gatehouse, Cartmel* The little town of Cartmel, 15 miles from Lancaster and seven from Ulverston 'over sands', as a signpost built into a wall puts it, is in fact two townships, divided by the River Ea, which runs through it. The Square and the priory gatehouse are in Upper Holker (pronounced 'hooker'), the church and the rest of the village in Lower Allithwaite. The 14th century gatehouse is all that remains of the priory. Once its upper storey housed the grammar school, now it is an artist's studio. Holker Hall, home of the George Preston who did so much for the Priory Church and now owned by the Cavendish family, is a mile or two north-west of Cartmel, but only the Old Wing remains of the early 17th century building. A rebuilding after a fire in 1871 has produced a magnificent extravaganza in Victorian Elizabethan.

42

*Cartmel Priory Church* Chance preserved Cartmel priory church from destruction during the Dissolution. When William Marshall, later the 2nd Earl of Pembroke, founded the priory for the Augustinian Canons in 1188, he stipulated that, in the monks' church, an altar with a priest should be provided for the people, who would always have the right to worship in that part of the priory church. So King Henry VIII's Commissioners, when they came to ransack the priory, had to agree that the Chapel of St Michael was the parish church, and spared it. The ruin of the rest of the church was rebuilt during the following century, through the munificence of George Preston, of Holker Hall, who gave the black oak screen and canopies to match the 15th century stalls. The tower, with its diagonally set top storey, is said to be architecturally unsound, but it has stood firm for 500 years.

*Fell Foot, Windermere* Fell Foot, at the lower end of Windermere, is the gateway to a country park. A mile or so down the road the swift River Leven passes under the 17th century Newby Bridge. It is built of Lakeland slate and its five uneven arches and sharply pointed buttresses are a piquant contast to the folly known as the Pennington Tower which rises out of the woods behind. In the hills to the north-east of Fell Foot is one of the rarest churches in Lakeland. St Anthony's Cartmel Fell, built at the beginning of the 16th century, has a three-decker pulpit dating from 1698 and, even more exceptional, the mutilated torso of a wooden crucified Christ, believed to be 13th century. Mrs Humphrey (*East Lynne*) Ward took Cartmel church as the model for Browhead Chapel in her novel *Helbeck of Bannisdale.*

46

*Windermere, near Gummer's How* Lancashire can claim only part of the east bank of Windermere, and so not the town, which is in traditional Westmorland, but there are no territorial disputes over the view from this point near the southern end of the lake, looking north-west towards Borrowdale. It belongs to all.

Windermere, 10½ miles long and, in places, so narrow as to look like a river, is England's largest lake. Is that why this inland area should have put up Finsthwaite Tower, in the woods behind Lakeside Station, 'to honour the officers, seamen and marines of the Royal Navy whose matchless conduct and irresistible valour decisively defeated the fleets of France, Spain and Holland, and promoted and protected liberty and commerce, 1799.'

It was on Windermere that, in 1930, Sir Henry Segrave died while breaking the world record for speed boats by touching 98¾mph.

*Esthwaite Water and Roger Ground*
Esthwaite Water, smaller and less invaded by summer crowds than Windermere, into which it flows, was known and loved by Wordsworth from boyhood. This was the lake on whose surface, 'in the frosty season', as he recalls in *The Prelude*, the Hawkshead Grammar School boys *'hissed along the polished ice in games confederate, imitative of the chase'.*

The southern end of Esthwaite Water has associations with a lesser but perhaps more beloved artist-writer. Hill Top Farm, near Sawrey, a 17th century house, was the home for the last 30 years of her life of Beatrix Potter, less well known beyond the Lake District as Mrs Heelis, a successful farmer and sheep-breeder. She left her house to the National Trust and, in summer, visitors can see a collection of the possessions of the creator of Peter Rabbit, Mrs Tiggywinkle, Pigling Bland and the rest.

*The Grammar School, Hawkshead*   At Hawkshead, Wordsworth spent his happy schoolboy years, boarding at Ann Tyson's cottage which still stands in the village, in a lane running off the square opposite the Red Lion. The desk on which he carved his name is shown to visitors, but the foundation which Edwin Sandys, Archbishop of York, endowed in 1585 is no longer a school. The doorway, with a sundial above it, dates from 1675. On the right of the Grammar School is a glimpse of the tower of St Michael's Church, with the tomb of the Archbishop's parents, William and Margaret Sandys, in the north-east corner.

*Coniston Water, from Brantwood* Brantwood, on the east shore of Coniston Water, is the house where John Ruskin lived from 1871 until his death in 1900. It was he who laid out with flowering shrubs the grounds that run for a mile beside the lake, with a view across it to the stern slopes of the Old Man of Coniston, 2,635ft high. Ruskin's grave is in Coniston churchyard: it was by his own wish that he lies there, under a cross of the hard green Lakeland stone, rather than in Westminster Abbey. In the museum at Coniston there are a number of his early drawings, along with relics ranging from a lock of his hair and his geological hammer to the Bible from which his mother taught him.

*View towards Dunnerdale* The higher road from Broughton-in-Furness to Hall Dunnerdale and Seathorpe is a memorably scenic stretch. The first stage runs between Stickle Pike on the left, Brown Haw and Brock Barrow on the right, the second drops back into the steep valley of the Duddon. The small church at Seathwaite, built with money given by H. W. Schneider, the Barrow ironmaster, replaces the chapel where, for 67 years, Robert Walker was the incumbent. For Wordsworth he was 'A Pastor such as Chaucer's verse portrays'. Between Sunday services he assembled his flock beneath a churchyard yew and ministered to their material needs. On an extremely modest stipend he brought up and educated eight children. Most remarkably, when he died at the age of 93, he left £2,000, saved from the profits of farming his glebe, shearing his own sheep and carrying to market the wool he spun.

*River Duddon South of Ulpha*

*The Kirk of Ulpha to the pilgrim's eye*
*Is welcome as a star, that doth present*
*Its shining forehead through the peaceful*
*rent*
*Of a black cloud diffused o'er half the*
*sky'*

So wrote Wordworth, in one of the sonnets inspired by his beloved Duddon Valley, and since Ulpha (locally 'oofa') was the junction of the fell road to Eskdale it was probably true enough for 19th century travellers. All 34 sonnets were needed to convey the variety of the River Duddon which, rising near the Three Shire Stone at the head of the Wrynose Pass, the point where Lancashire, Westmorland and Cumberland meet, comes down in curves and falls, through cleft and gorge before finding its way through marshes and flats to the Irish Sea

between Millom and Walney Island.

*Furness Abbey, Barrow-in-Furness* These walls and pillars of ruddy sandstone, built in the 'Vale of Deadly Nightshade', a mile or two north-east of Barrow, are all that remains of Furness Abbey, which Stephen, Count of Mortmain, later to be King Stephen, founded in 1123. Originally it belonged to the Order of Savigny, but in 1147 it became Cistercian. The Cistercians, whose houses were invariably built in lonely spots and by running water, were notable farmers and cultivators, renowned for clearing forests and taming the wilderness. By the 13th century they controlled the whole of the Furness peninsula and, at the Dissolution of the monasteries under Henry VIII, the abbey ranked as one of the most important religious houses in the north. Its destruction was thorough; the lead was stripped from the roofs and the buildings were 'cannibalised' to provide stone for local farms and churches.

*Barrow-in-Furness* Today Barrow-in-Furness, with its docks and shipyards, which Gladstone, when he opened the first dock in 1867, called 'the youngest child of England's enterprise', might be 30 instead of three or so miles away from peaceful Rampside Sands. But in the mid-19th century it, like Barrow, had jetties to ship iron ore which the Furness Railway brought from the mines in the Dalton district. Off-

shore is the low-lying Piel Island, with the ruins of a medieval castle which was built to defend the coast route to Furness Abbey from Scottish raiders. It failed to repel the pretender, Lambert Simnel, in 1487; he held court in the keep as 'Edward IV'. Little less remote, given the present calm of Piel Island, seems the fact that, until 1882, Piel Pier, long demolished, was the main terminus for passenger ships leaving Barrow.

*Morecambe Bay and Arnside Knott* Today
the railway runs round Morecambe Bay and
sailing craft skim across it. In the 19th
century, according to a directory of 1849,
Arnside Sands were 'covered one hour with
ships and another with carriages and
pedestrians.' For centuries the usual way
from Lancashire to the Furness peninsula
had been over the sands. Cartmel Priory had
a special responsibility for the bay, pro-
viding a guide for a journey made perilous
by the swift tides and the constantly chang-
ing channels of the rivers flowing into it.
After the Dissolution the Duchy of Lancaster
had oversight of the bay, but, even so,
between the 16th and the late 19th
centuries, more than 140 travellers were
drowned and buried on Cartmel Priory land.
Nowadays crossings are made only for
pleasure, on foot and at times when the
guide is certain that the shifting course of
the River Kent is favourable.

*Old Canal, Borwick* Today the upper reaches of the disused Lancaster Canal are so charmingly pastoral that it is hard to envisage the part it played in the Industrial Revolution. It was in 1792 that Lancaster businessmen engaged in the West Indies trade raised the money to build a canal that would carry the coal from Wigan up to Westmorland, and, incidentally, carry back the lime with which to dress the acid soil of South Lancashire. The engineer they engaged was the notable John Rennie, who also built the Ulverston sea canal, and who, at Lancaster, carried his canal across the Lune in an elegant aqueduct. Later he was reproached for overspending by doing so.

Borwick Hall, not far from the canal, is an Elizabethan house of about 1590-95 incorporating a 14th century peel tower.

*Brunton Lathe* The wide horizons of the Forest of Bowland — and here we are at its heart — have been compared to the open sea in their vastness. Looking today at the bare hill pastures it is hard to believe that, long ago, the Lancashire hills were wooded up to, or above, a thousand feet. Every acre of grassland here has been won by settlers, working often with primitive tools. There are areas where that history can be read in the lack of villages and the presence of isolated farmsteads, the homes of early colonists who hacked out their holdings from the wild and enclosed them.

*Bridge over the River Hodder, Higher Whitewell* The Hodder Valley valley is relatively soft country, and our remote ancestors evidently found it congenial. Pieces of Bronze Age pottery have been found in Fairy Holes cave, near Whitewell. Further down the valley, a little south of Chipping, which, though no more than a village, was a market as long ago as the 13th century, there is a farmhouse where those who run may read. Richard Alston, who, in 1582, built himself Hesketh End, Hesketh Lane, gave it mullioned windows and a façade with a frieze on which are inscribed details of English history from the Romans to his own day.

*Forest of Bowland* Here we are at the gateway of the wild Lancashire which never fails to astonish visitors who have imagined the county to be wholly industrial. The Forest of Bowland is an outlier of the Pennines, a region of upland sheep farms with rugged moors above, cut by narrow, wooded valleys. The road through the Trough of Bowland, where the picture was taken, runs from west to east. There are no metalled roads over the moors that rise on either hand but the Roman Road along which, in 79AD Agricola marched his legionaries from Mamucium, now Manchester, to Carlisle, can be traced over the north-eastern fells. He took the high road because he found the bleak moorland less hostile than the natives, the Brigantes.

*Packhorse Bridge, River Hodder* The graceful old packhorse bridge over the River Hodder, a mile or so before it flows in the Ribble, dates from 1563, and was apparently built by public subscription. We know the name of the mason; Roger Crossley was paid £70 for building it, or, more probably, organising its building, since he was unlikely to have worked single-handed. Today the traffic from Stonyhurst to Clitheroe crosses the river by a neighbouring bridge, constructed in 1826, when the Scottish engineer, John McAdam, was rebuilding the road from Longridge to Clitheroe. It was here that he made one of his early experiments with the road surface made up of layers of small stones bound with tar or asphalt which still bears his name.

74

*Great Mitton* Less than two miles west of this stretch of the Ribble the cupolas of Lancashire's grandest Elizabethan mansion rise above its monumental gatehouse. There was a house on the site of Stonyhurst College in the 14th century, when the Shireburns were already lords of the manor. Building on the Elizabethan house was started by Sir Richard Shireburn, and continued by his son, another Sir Richard. A 17th century Shireburn, Sir Nicholas, engaged the royal gardener, Henry Wise, to lay out the gardens and the majestic approach. After that came a change of ownership and a period of neglect until, in 1794, Thomas Weld, the owner, gave the house to the Society of Jesus for the English College, originally at St Omer, which had been driven out of Liège by the French Revolution. The treasures owned by the school include Henry VII's cope, which his son, Henry VIII, wore at the Field of the Cloth of Gold.

*The Gatehouse, Whalley* First churchyard, then church, finally the ancient-seeming ruins of the Cistercian abbey — the chronology of Whalley's monuments deceives the eye. In the churchyard there are three preaching crosses of the kind which Christian congregations in Saxon England set up to mark a place of worship until they could afford to build a church. An Anglo-Saxon and later a Norman church rose beside them, but the present St Mary's Church is 13th and 15th century, retaining only a Norman south doorway. The interior has 15th century stalls, with superb misericords, which came from the abbey. The abbey itself, whose gracious ruin is near the church, was built at the very end of the 13th century and the conventual buildings and the north-east gateway, by which one enters the grounds, not until the middle and the end respectively of the 15th.

*Downham* Downham is a village that might have been transported from, or, without alteration, might be transported to the Cotswolds. Its main street runs uphill to the 15th century church tower where hang three bells from Whalley Abbey. In Downham Park, nearby, the Roman road marches on its way from Ribchester to Ilkley. South of the village Pendle Hill rises to 1,800ft. Popular history associates the area with the 'Lancashire Witches', a few pitiful old women who, in the reign of James I, were victims of one of the periodic attacks of hysteria about witchcraft and suffered death by burning. Harrison Ainsworth wrote a novel about them, but a better memory for the breezy top of Pendle Hill is of Quaker George Fox looking down from its summit at the good farmland below and noting the places where the Lord had 'a great people to be gathered.'

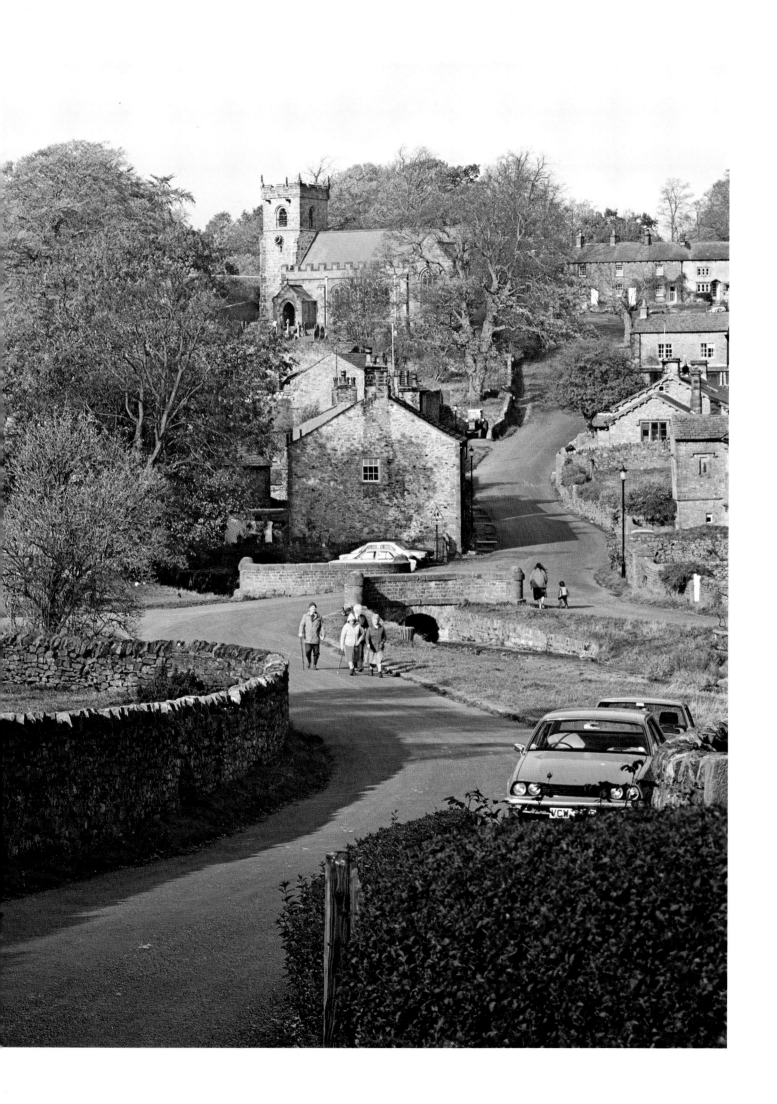

*Wycoller* Lying in a remote hollow of the moors barely five miles north-east of industrial Nelson, Wycoller has seven bridges over the stream that runs through it. One, a packhorse bridge, is said to be 13th century. Nobody can guess at the age of that in the picture, a single slab of stone secured by boulders on either bank. Wycoller Hall, a 16th-17th century house, now in ruins, is in Brontë country. This was the model for the 'Ferndean Manor' of Charlotte Brontë's *Jane Eyre*. It was to an idealised version of the house that her heroine made her way to be reunited with that very type of romantic heroes, the blind Rochester, and to find that now he was free to marry her.

*Canal Wharf, Burnley* A textile town with an ancient past; Burnley's market rights go back to 1243, when the farmers of the Pendle district brought their produce here and spinning and weaving lay centuries ahead. The pride of Burnley is Townley Hall, originally the home of the Townley family, which now houses the museum and art gallery. Once a strong point of the 14th century, the house as we see it today dates variously from the 17th, 18th and early 19th centuries. There are fine stuccos in the Great Hall and fine 15th and 16th century woodwork in the chapel, which, in the 18th century, was transferred piece by piece from the east range to its present position. To Charles Townley, a collector of antique statuary, who died in 1805, the British Museum owes the Townley Marbles.

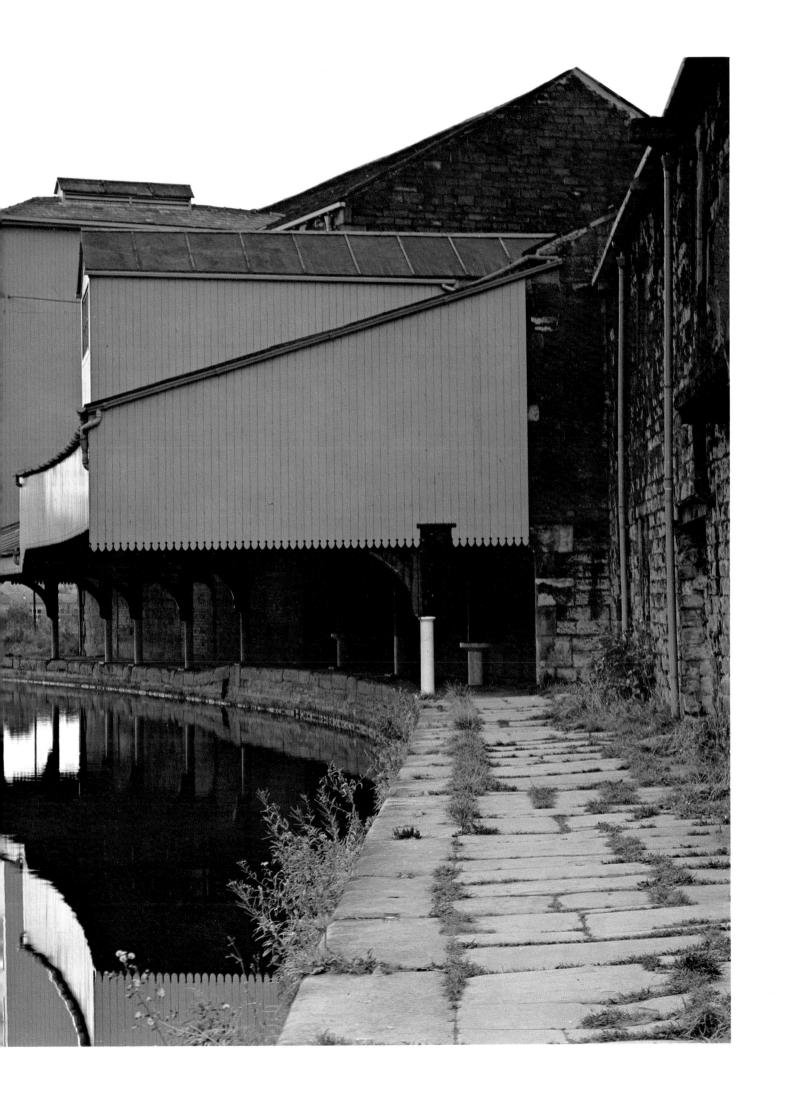

*Gawthorpe Hall, Padiham* Gawthorpe Hall was built between 1600-7 round an existing peel tower — such strong points were needed in the turbulent north well into the Middle Ages — and remained unaltered until the mid-19th century, when Sir Charles Barry made it look rather more Elizabethan as well as modernising the interior. Happily he did not tamper with the plaster friezes and ceilings. The Rev Lawrence Shuttleworth, who built the hall, kept the household accounts, and we can read in detail of the work of 17th century plasterers and masons, glaziers and joiners. Gawthorpe remained in the Shuttleworth family until 1970 and its last occupant, the late Rachel Kay-Shuttleworth, made it a show case for fine embroidery. It is now the property of the National Trust.

*Longridge Fell, viewed from Kemple End*
Longridge Fell, rising to more than 1,100ft, is a grandstand for viewing some of the most attractive countryside in North Lancashire, besides being the quarry from which the elegant grey stone houses of Lancaster were built. Five miles or so south west of Kemple End is Ribchester, the Roman Bremetennacum, whose 13th century church stands on the site of a Roman fort. Two pillars supporting the west gallery of the church are said to have come from the fort. Near the churchyard gate there is a museum showing many of the finds made by four or five generations of archaeologists, with, behind it, the Roman granaries, excavated and on show. The fertile Ribble valley, overlooked from this spot at Kemple End, was popular with pensioned-off legionaries. Some of today's farmers may have distant Roman ancestors.

*Eanan Wharf, Blackburn* Once Blackburn was the biggest cotton town in the world. They were weaving here in the 16th century: in the 20th the town had 80,000 looms and mill chimneys unnumbered. It was in one of the cottages where the old handlooms were set up that James Hargreaves invented the spinning jenny, which led to his being driven out of his native town by his workmates, who saw it as a threat to their livelihood. The wharf, with its tall warehouses that have a hint of Holland, is on the Leeds-Liverpool Canal, here a very different waterway from that along which 18th century passengers accomplished their leisurely voyages from Liverpool to Wigan.

*Hoghton Tower, near Preston* Hoghton Tower (pronounced Hawton), with its sloping mile-long drive and outer and inner courtyards, was built mainly during the late 16th century, but the Hoghton family have lived here since the early 14th and the present house is believed to have succeeded a fortress-mansion. It has known a period of decay — in the 18th century it was let in tenements to weavers — but today is restored and inhabited. Here James I is said to have given us the word sirloin by playfully knighting a joint of beef which had greatly pleased him when he was entertained at Hoghton in 1617. It is a pretty story, but, in fact, the word derives from the Old French *surlogne*, above the loin. What is true is that the king's host, Sir Richard Hoghton, spent so lavishly on entertaining his sovereign that he went bankrupt.

92

*Astley Hall, Chorley* One of the finest Renaissance houses in Lancashire, Astley Hall is remarkable also for the fact that it stands off the main street of an industrial town; the approach is through a public park. Its façade, with more glass than brick or stone, which dates from the 1660s, stands in front of a late 16th century timber house. The interior is equally striking, with bravura stucco decoration, which Pevsner calls 'barbaric in its very excesses', in the Great Hall and paintings of a rather odd assortment of great men, ranging from Tamerlane to William of Orange, along the panelling of the lower walls. The items shown to visitors include a bed in which Cromwell is reputed to have slept after the Battle of Preston.

*White Coppice, Chorley* Chorley is another Lancashire industrial centre with a 13th century past as a market town, and, to this day, it has escaped the worst scars of intensive development and has the country literally on its doorstep. The moors are within walking distance. It was the birthplace, in 1819, of Henry Tate, who devised the process of turning loaf sugar into cubes. It brought him a great deal of money and he spent it on giving the country the building and the endowment of the Tate Gallery, which stands on the site of the old Millbank Prison beside the Thames.

*Leeds and Liverpool Canal, Wigan* Wigan Pier is one of the oldest of music hall jokes. Wigan town can rise above it, having stood for 800, or 900 or even a thousand years on a site where, a thousand or so years before that, the Romans built a fort to guard a road junction. Its parish church is mentioned in Domesday Book and though the present building is mostly mid-19th century, it incorporates 13th century fragments. A Roman altar found in . 1847 beneath the communion table has been built into the tower. Wigan was already a textile town in the 18th century and, at the same period, famous for bell-founding, sending its rings as far afield as North Wales. To this day antiquarians prize Wigan pewter and Wigan grandfather clocks.

*Rivington Tower* Rivington Pike, where the 18th century tower stands almost 1,200ft above sea level, was an ancient beacon site; this was a link in the chain of fire that warned Elizabethan England of the approach of the Spanish Armada. The reservoir below it was built in the mid-19th century to supply Liverpool with water. Fifty years later the future Lord Leverhulme bought Rivington Hall, with land east of the reservoir, and laid it out as a public park for the people of Liverpool. In it he had built a replica of the 13th century church which once stood where Derby Square, Liverpool, now is, and also had restored two cruck barns, one 105ft long, which stand in the park.

*Leigh* Leigh has mill chimneys as the town of San Gimignano, in Tuscany, has towers, and some of them are impressive for more than mere height. Alder Mill, for example, done in red and yellow brick and terra cotta, is crowned by a copper cupola.

In the modern church of St Thomas there is a bishop's chair older than the town. A carved inscription tells us that it was made from beams which Norman carpenters had set in the roof of Winchester Cathedral. Leigh was the birthplace of Joseph Farington, a mediocre artist, though he was a power in the Royal Academy of the 18th century, whose reputation today rests on his copious diaries, which have established him as a provincial Pepys, though of less engaging personality.

*Bridgewater Canal, Worsley* One would hardly look for a model village in industrial south-east Lancashire, but Worsley, a green oasis on the outskirts of Salford and Swinton, has some claim to be called one. It owes its fine parish church, one of Gilbert Scott's earlier works, to the first Lord Ellesmere, and its place in history to his great-uncle, the third Duke of Bridgewater. In 1758-61 he financed the first cross-country canal in England to carry coal from his estates to Manchester, where its price was halved. 18th century tourists came to see the entrance to the mile-long tunnel, still visible, leading to the coal mines. The red sandstone of the canal's locks and bridges was hewn from the cliff through which the tunnel was driven.

*The Cathedral, Manchester* A new cathedral but an old church — though Manchester did not become the centre of the diocese until 1847, there was a church on this site at the time of the Domesday Survey. In 1421 it was refounded as a collegiate establishment served by a number of priests; the greater part of the present cathedral dates from the rebuilding that took place during the next hundred or so years. The canopied choir stalls, with their often comic misericords, compare with the best in Europe. Older Mancunians remember their cathedral soot-black, hemmed in by narrow streets. War damage and post-war town planning have opened up the spaces around it and the stone has been restored to its original colour. Today the medieval collegiate buildings house the boys and girls of Chetham's Hospital, once a charity school, now an independent grammar school for the musically gifted.

*Barton Arcade, Deansgate, Manchester*
The Victorians loved arcades, but none of them created a more striking one than this splendid three-decker off Deansgate, whose domes look down on shops and offices disposed on curving balconies as well as on ground level. A recent restoration has let us see the glass sparkling as when the arcade was built in 1871, at a cost of £25,000. Farther along Deansgate there is an architectural contrast in the Rylands Library,

built in the most elaborate late 19th century Gothic. Rich in precious MSS and early printed books, it is a memorial to one of Manchester's enlighted cotton magnates, John Rylands. Continue to the far end of the street and, among the railway arches near the Rochdale Canal, you will find a fragment of wall built when Manchester was a Roman station from which seven roads radiated.

*Barton-upon-Irwell* Barton Bridge is a modern industrial spectacular, with its remarkable grouping in a relatively small area of swing bridge, power station, transformer station and the M62 motorway flying over the Manchester Ship Canal. The swing bridge is in fact an acqueduct, carrying the Bridgewater Canal, and is believed to be unique. The centre section can be sealed to form a tank, and swings open when big vessels are passing along the Ship Canal. It was here that James Brindley, the brilliant self-taught engineer, said to have been unable to read or write, who worked for the 'Canal Duke', built his first acqueduct to carry the Bridgewater Canal over the Irwell Navigation. Barton Town, a little to the north, has an unusual neighbouring of Anglican and RC churches. The latter, which was the gift of the Trafford family, is considered to be the best work of E. W. Pugin, son of the great A. W. N. Pugin, the apostle of Victorian Gothic.

# Index

Barrow-in-Furness, Furness Abbey   60
Barrow-in-Furness   62
Barton upon Irwell   110
Blackburn, Eanan Wharf   90
Blackpool, Tower & Pier   30
Blackpool, Illuminations   28
Borwick   66
Bowland, Trough of   72
Brunton, Lathe   68
Burnley, Canal Wharf   84
Burscough Bridge   20

Cartmel, Market Cross   42
Cartmel, Priory Church   44
Chorley, Astley Hall   94
Chorley, White Coppice   96
Coniston Water   54
Croston, River Yarrow   22

Downham   80
Duddon, River   58
Dunnesdale   56

Esthwaite Water   50

Fleetwood   32

Great Mutton   76

Hawkshead, Grammar School   52
Hodder, River   70
Hodder, River, Packhorse Bridge   74

Lancaster   36
Lancaster, Old Custom House   38
Leigh   102
Liverpool, from Birkenhead   10
Liverpool, Cathedral   12
Liverpool, St George's Hall   18
Liverpool, Rodney Street   14
Liverpool, Walker Art Gallery   16
Longridge Fell   88
Lytham St Annes   26

Manchester, Cathedral   106
Manchester, Barton Arcade   108
Morecambe Bay   64

Padiham, Gawthorpe Hall   86
Preston, Harris Museum   24
Preston, Hoghton Tower   92

Rivington Tower   100

Silverdale   40

Thurnham   34

Whalley, Gatehouse   78
Widnes, Runcorn Bridge   8
Wigan   98
Windermere, Fell Foot   46
Windermere, Gummer's How   48
Worsley   104
Wycoller   82